MINNESOTA'S IRISH

MINNESOTA'S IRISH

PATRICIA CONDON JOHNSTON

JOHNSTON PUBLISHING INC., AFTON, MINNESOTA

Also by Patricia Condon Johnston
Stillwater: Minnesota's Birthplace
Eastman Johnson's Lake Superior Indians
Address inquiries to:
Johnston Publishing Inc.
Box 96
Afton, MN 55001

for Charlie

CONTENTS

PREFACE

This book grew out of a longtime fascination with my own Irish heritage. My Condon great-grandparents were children in County Cork, Ireland, during the famine years in the 1840s. Most of Minnesota's Irish share a similar legacy. It is only fair to point out that I am also mainly concerned with the Catholic Irish. This is simply because, culturally and historically, the Protestant Irish and the Catholic Irish have had little in common. Most of the Irish immigrants who came to Minnesota were Catholic.

My particular interest in Ellen Ireland, the archbishop's sister, was probably first aroused in the late 1950s when I graduated from St. Joseph's Academy in the Ellen Ireland Auditorium. (Following a tradition that dated to Ellen Ireland's time, each of the nearly two hundred girls in our class wore floor-length white dresses and carried a dozen long-stemmed red roses.) Years later when I received a grant from the National Endowment for the Humanities to write a series of articles concerning significant Minnesotans for *Minnesota History,* I chose Ellen Ireland as one of my subjects.

At best, she was a difficult person to research. Seventy-two years of her life had been spent as a Sister of St. Joseph. Though she ranked alongside her brother in the Catholic community, she did not want her life remembered and in fact fastidiously destroyed her correspondence. (This was typical of nuns until recently; having chosen a life of penance and service, they were discouraged from keeping any personal memorabilia including letters or photographs.) Much of the material I used for my article, ''Reflected Glory: The Story of Ellen Ireland'' *(Minnesota History,* Spring, 1982), was gleaned from oral history interviews conducted by Sister Ann Thomasine Sampson, Director of Community Oral History Project for the Sisters of St. Joseph of Carondelet, St. Paul Province. Portions of this article are reprinted in *Minnesota's Irish* with the permission of the Minnesota Historical Society.

Several other people deserve special recognition for their help with this book. The first of these is Jim Rogers, a student of Irish American history who lives in St. Paul. Jim wrote the chapter on boxing, "The Fighting Irish," read manuscript for me, and suggested many sources for information and photographs. One of the people he introduced me to was Father John Berger, originally from Green Isle, Minnesota, who compiled a history of that community in the 1960s. Father Berger supplied numerous photographs from Green Isle. One windy Sunday afternoon last autumn, he also took my husband, Charlie, and me to Jessenland, the site of the first Irish farming settlement in Minnesota. The Doheny brothers who founded it are among Father Berger's Irish ancestors.

Margaret Anne Mindrum, whose great-great-grandfather was Dillon O'Brien, helped with O'Brien family history and photographs. Philip Donnelly, who is related to both Dillon O'Brien and Ignatius Donnelly, likewise provided information and photographs.

I am also especially grateful to Dr. Matthew J. Bruccoli, the author of *Some Sort of Epic Grandeur* and several other books concerning F. Scott Fitzgerald, for the portrait photograph of the St. Paul writer. The photograph of Scott Fitzgerald with his father, Edward Fitzgerald, is from the Papers of F. Scott Fitzgerald, Princeton University Library.

Additional photographs were obtained from my mother, Betty Condon, my grandmother, Hortense Braaten, Bill and Mary Catherine Davern, Lydia Wulff, Mae Mach, Dolly Brazil, Dan Gibbons, Mike Fitzgerald, Sister Mary Kraft at the Archives of the Sisters of St. Joseph of Carondelet, St. Paul Province, John Davenport at the College of St. Thomas, and the Irish American Cultural Institute.

Dale Johnston, a partner with Charlie and me in Johnston Publishing, is responsible for the singular beauty of *Minnesota's Irish*. He also designed our two earlier books: *Stillwater, Minnesota's Birthplace* and *Eastman Johnson's Lake Superior Indians.*

My husband, Charlie, of course, is both mentor and helpmate to me. His enthusiasm for this book made it possible. He also took the photograph of the Church of St. Thomas and its cemetery in Jessenland and copied about a dozen photographs for *Minnesota's Irish* from originals in the Archives of the Catholic Historical Society in St. Paul. Once again (though he's only Irish by marriage), this book is dedicated to him.

Davern Street in St. Paul is named for William Quin Davern, pictured here in 1906 with his wife, Catherine, and twelve of their thirteen children and their families. The empty chair on the right was for another son, Mathew, who had not been seen or heard from since he left home sixteen years earlier for Alaska during the Klondike gold rush.

Born in County Clare, Ireland, William Davern was farming in what became Highland Park in 1850. His 160-acre claim was bounded by the present Snelling, Montreal, Fairview, and St. Paul avenues.

ST. PAUL'S IRISH IMAGE

Minnesota's capital city brags of its Irish beginnings and rightly so. In 1839 the first settlers to claim land in what became downtown St. Paul were a pair of Irish soldiers, Edward Phelan and John Hays. Phelan had been mustered out of the army at Fort Snelling where Hays was waiting for his discharge. They took up adjoining claims below the present Kellogg Boulevard, extending from Minnesota to Eagle streets and from the river back to the bluff. In his partner's absence, Phelan built a log house, a hovel of sorts, which the two shared later that summer.

There's a good deal more to the story, however. John Hays, poor soul, was the first man murdered in St. Paul. Possibly, Phelan did the deed. It was true that the men had little in common. Phelan was a giant of a man, well over six feet tall, with a reputation for being "immoral, cruel, revengeful, and unscrupulous." Still in his twenties, he was from Londonderry, Ireland, and had enlisted in the army in New York City in 1835. Hays was a smaller man and several years his senior. War Department records show him to be just under five feet, nine inches tall, and

forty years old. Born in Waterford, Ireland, he was well-liked by those who knew him and praised as "an honest, good, courteous, and clever old gentleman." He was also a frugal man, never married, who had put away a tidy sum of money during several terms in the service.

When John Hays mysteriously disappeared in September, 1839, it was only natural that a finger be pointed at Phelan. The latter claimed he had no idea as to his companion's whereabouts. But after Hays's body washed up near Carver's Cave with his head bashed in, Phelan was arrested for murder.

There was little doubt among his neighbors as to the suspect's guilt. One woman said that Phelan had told her a short time before that he and Hays were getting on "very badly," but that he would "soon be rid of him." Another settler testified that he had seen blood on Phelan's clothes and that bloodstained clothing was found under the floor in his cabin. In addition, the man said, his dog had sniffed out the scene of the murder near the cabin and traced the path by which the body was dragged to the river.

Nonetheless, when Phelan stood trial for murder in Prairie du Chien (the seat of Crawford County, Wisconsin Territory, which included St. Paul at the time), a jury failed to convict him and he was set free. Several years later a Dakota warrior confessed that he had been the one who killed Hays. Whatever the truth, Phelan returned to St. Paul and moved to a new claim on the creek that now bears his name. (The spelling has been changed to Phalen.) Years later, given enough rope, he got what most of St. Paul thought he had coming to him.

In the spring of 1850 the first grand jury to sit in Ramsey County indicted Phelan for perjury. The sheriff was sent to apprehend him, but Phelan had already fled for California. En route, while crossing the plains, he was murdered by fellow travelers. His behavior had been so barbarous and overbearing, they contended, that they had been compelled to kill him in self-defense. Historian J. Fletcher Williams, writing in 1876, applauded this fitting application of frontier justice. Convinced in his own mind of Phelan's duplicity, Williams called it a disgrace "that the name of this brutal murderer has been affixed to one of our most beautiful lakes—one that supplies our households with water."

So much for St. Paul's Irish origins. But the Irish indeed overcame. Relegating this blackguard's skeleton to the closet, they soon stamped St. Paul with the Irish label it carries to the present day. They did this, amazingly enough, despite being outnumbered by their German neighbors. While the Germans made up the predominant ethnic group in St. Paul, the immigrant Irish had a couple of advantages. Their familiarity with the English language and Anglo-American culture was one. Secondly, they were born politicians.

Gravitating as they did early on to civil service jobs, the Irish were quick to see the political arena as a birthing place for upward social mobility. For a man with the right talents, a career in politics required a minimum of education, preparation, or money. In this respect, it had much the same appeal as prizefighting where St. Paul Irish also came to glory. In 1858 six of the city's eleven policemen were Irish (causing complaints from the Germans). Twenty years later, though the Irish accounted for only ten percent of the city's work force, one in three police officers was from Ireland. St. Paul's first Irish mayor in 1878 was William Dawson, a successful banker born in County Cavan, Ireland. When another Irishman, Christopher O'Brien, was elected to that office in 1883, St. Paul found itself in for a rude awakening.

This early Cathedral on Wabasha and Sixth streets in St. Paul, built in 1851, was a combination church, residence, and school. The bishop, clergy, and seminarians occupied the third floor, the church was on the second floor, and the first floor or basement contained a library, kitchen, dining room, and school rooms.

Up until then, under mostly Yankee mayors, the city had controlled vice by supervising it. O'Brien would have none of this, but insisted on enforcing the laws he had sworn to uphold. By doing so, said an 1899 history of the police and fire departments, he proved that "a great city can flourish apart from periodical fees paid it for tolerance of vice in its midst." A later source recalled that O'Brien "suppressed vice wherever he found it, with the result that it was continually cropping up in unexpected places."

Admittedly, there was considerable backsliding from this position on the part of a later Irish politician or two. In the first years of this century, a pair of brothers, Richard and James O'Connor, were responsible for the infamous "O'Connor System." Richard was one of the most influential Democrats in the country. James was Chief of Police in St. Paul for nineteen years beginning in 1901. Their bargain with the underworld guaranteed wanted criminals protection in St. Paul so long as they behaved themselves in the city. These were the days when Nina Clifford's house of prostitution was just around the corner from the police station. Predictably, the scheme eventually backfired. Following a spree of spectacular kidnappings in the early 1930s, St. Paul was exposed in the national press as a "hotbed of crime."

Even so, voter enthusiasm for Irish candidates remained high in St. Paul. One reason was that Irish politicians, here and elsewhere, have always prided themselves on taking care of their own. They also usually supported public works projects, providing employment for their constituents. As late as 1957 a study concluded that being Catholic was "almost essential for political success in St. Paul." The city's Irish, assuredly, form the largest block of Catholics. This bias has abated somewhat in recent years, but gaggles of Irish names are still the rule on local ballots.

As the seat of a sizable Catholic archdiocese, St. Paul also became the center of Irish religious activity in Minnesota. This was of no small consequence. In Minnesota, as in America at large, Catholicism has played a major role in the history and culture of the Irish community. Even those Irish who turned their backs on their faith or attempted to ignore it (F. Scott Fitzgerald is a good hometown example) have been deeply influenced by it. Mother Church has helped shape the Irish character, and the Irish, for their part, have helped shape Mother Church. The single most outstanding figure in the Catholic Church in Minnesota (and one of the most colorful prelates in the history of the American hierarchy) was St. Paul's first archbishop, John Ireland.

John Ireland was St. Paul's first archbishop and a dominant figure in the religious, social, and political life of the United States for more than half a century. The archbishop of Philadelphia once called him the "consecrated blizzard of the Northwest."

Founded by John Ireland in 1885, the College of St. Thomas began as the St. Thomas Aquinas Seminary for ecclesiastical and lay students, teaching theology, philosophy, and six-year classical courses. Reverend Thomas O'Gorman was the first president. The seminary department was transferred to the new St. Paul Seminary in 1894.

Born in the village of Burnchurch, County Kilkenny, Ireland, on September 11, 1838, John Ireland was the second of six children of Richard and Judith Naughton Ireland and their first son. The Irelands were among the hundreds of thousands of Irish people who abandoned their homeland during the mid-1800s because of the potato famines. One of Richard's sisters and her husband, Anastasia and James Howard, had already perished, adding four orphaned children to the Ireland household. In 1849, bent on finding a better life for his expanded family, Richard sailed for America. He was accompanied by one of the Howard children and an unmarried sister, Nancy Ireland, who would raise the young Howards. The next year, after he found work in Burlington, Vermont, Judith joined him in Boston's harbor with all nine of the remaining Ireland and Howard children in tow.

Like many another Irish family that stayed briefly on the East coast before pushing inland, the Irelands spent a year in Vermont. This was time enough for them to become caught up in the western migration movement which brought them by covered wagon to Chicago. John was enrolled at St. Mary's School, but the family didn't stay put for long. One day on a Chicago street, Richard met an old friend from Ireland, John O'Gorman, who convinced him to move his family to Minnesota.

The new territory was being touted as a health resort and an agricultural paradise. Traveling by prairie schooner to Galena, the O'Gormans and the Irelands boarded the steamboat *Nominee* bound for St. Paul. They docked at the Jackson Street levee on May 20, 1852, and the Irelands lived at first in a hastily-built shack Richard put up for them at Fifth and St. Peter streets. Soon afterwards, he purchased a lot and erected a sturdy five-room house on Pearl Street (now West Fifth Street) between Washington and Market.

Family life at the Irelands' centered on the church even more so than in most Catholic households. Richard Ireland was a skilled carpenter who worked on Catholic construction projects in the city including the three-story stone Catholic Block, built in 1859 for store rental space on Third Street (now Kellogg Boulevard) between Cedar and Minnesota. (He also built many fine St. Paul residences.) Bishop Joseph Cretin, St. Paul's first bishop, was a friend of the family, and young John served Mass for him at the Cathedral where he also attended school. This early Cathedral was a three-story brick structure dating to 1851 on Wabasha and Sixth streets that housed the church, a residence for clergy and seminarians, and a parish school for boys. John's classmate and lifelong friend was Thomas O'Gorman (who later became bishop of the Sioux Falls diocese).

In 1853 Bishop Cretin arranged for these two boys to go to France to study for the priesthood. They were St. Paul's first seminarians. Bishop Cretin was from France and their schooling was provided free of cost at the seminaries where he had been trained. Eight years later, completing his studies before O'Gorman, John Ireland returned to St. Paul where he was ordained by Bishop Thomas Grace, Bishop Cretin's successor. The ceremony took place on December 21, 1861, in St. Paul's new Cathedral, a larger, more pretentious stone edifice completed in 1858 on Sixth Street at St. Peter. In the years that followed, until his death at the age of eighty in 1918, John Ireland's influence was felt worldwide.

As a young priest, Father Ireland served briefly (and heroically) in the Civil War as chaplain to the Fifth Minnesota Regiment, an Irish unit that is remembered for saving the day at Corinth, Mississippi. (A painting of the battle of Corinth in the Minnesota State Capitol includes a conspicuous portrait of Ireland.) Returning to St. Paul, as pastor at the Cathedral, he became a leader in the temperance movement. There was no doubt at the time that intoxicating drink was ruining many a good Irishman. As the story goes, John Ireland was prompted to immediate action one winter evening in 1869 when three men, surely under the influence, called on him at the Cathedral and thrust a crumpled piece of paper in his hand. "For God's sake, organize a Temperance Society," it read, followed by the signatures of seven men including a saloonkeeper. At the height of the movement a few years later not a single Irish Catholic name appeared over a saloon door in St. Paul.

As bishop of the St. Paul diocese in the 1870s, John Ireland undertook a mammoth colonization program which enabled thousands of Irish Catholic families to acquire farmsteads of their own in southwestern Minnesota. Many of their descendants remain in the communities he established. Once elevated to the archbishopric when the Archdiocese of St. Paul (which included all of Minnesota and Dakota Territory) was created in 1888, he gave his energies likewise to national and international affairs.

On the homefront, John Ireland lobbied for better wages for workers, religious instruction in the public schools, and an end to racial prejudice. (A frequent visitor at the White House, he knew and liked presidents Harrison, McKinley, Roosevelt, and Taft, but had little time for Woodrow Wilson whom he considered an opportunist and a bigot.) Taking on global responsibilities, in one instance, he helped smooth the takeover of the Catholic Philippine Islands by the United States in the wake of the Spanish-American War. Another Minnesotan, Supreme Court Justice Pierce Butler called Archbishop Ireland "a giant on the side of right in every crisis, in peace and war."

In St. Paul, Archbishop Ireland founded the College of St. Thomas in 1885 and the St. Paul Seminary in 1894. Both were built on the former 450-acre farm bordering the Mississippi River owned by Irishman William Finn. The seminary was the gift of James J. Hill whose wife, Mary Mehegan Hill, was the daughter of Irish immigrants. The archbishop also installed St. Paul's first electric streetcar system, the Grand Avenue line in 1890, to provide transportation out to the two schools.

The crowning achievement of John Ireland's long episcopate, and his most ambitious building project, was the present St. Paul Cathedral, designed by French architect Emmanuel Masqueray, and begun in 1906. When its cornerstone was laid the next year an estimated sixty thousand visitors thronged the city for the historic event. Catholicism had come of age in Minnesota. In 1907 the archbishop also broke ground for the Basilica of St. Mary in Minneapolis.

On September 11, 1938, the centenary of John Ireland's birth, a bronze plaque in his memory was installed in the Basilica. It includes a portrait of the archbishop in bas relief, garlanded with laurel leaves, and also his coat of arms. Displayed on the shield is a Dakota Indian in feathered headdress and blanket with his left hand on the hilt of a sword and his right hand holding a cross aloft. The motto reads: "Omnibus Omnia Factus Sum" (I Became All Things to All Men).

John and Mary White Condon were both born in County Cork, Ireland, and married after coming to this country in the 1850s. Like many of Minnesota's Irish, they lived in the East (in New Hampshire) for two or three years before coming West. The couple had ten children and farmed near Winona, but were twice reduced to penury, first by a tornado and then by a fire. Even so, when John Condon died in 1908, he left three houses in Winona and eleven thousand dollars.

GREEN VALLEYS

The first Irish in Minnesota were probably lumberjacks who had emigrated from Ireland to New Brunswick and Maine in the 1820s and 1830s. After government treaties signed with the native Dakota and Ojibwe Indians opened the timber-rich delta between the St. Croix and the Mississippi rivers to white ownership in 1837, these loggers entered Minnesota. By 1850 there were 263 Irish-born people in the territory, concentrated in Ramsey, Hennepin, Dakota, and Washington counties.

Some of these newcomers were farmers or laborers, but more than a third of the men were enlisted as soldiers at Forts Snelling and Ripley. These had already earned a reputation as rowdies. One disgusted German soldier wrote home in 1849: "Then we have many Irish in our company, from whom we have to bear much; when they are intoxicated, they knock everything down and want to do nothing but fight; the guardhouse is always full of them." The Irish women were mainly wives and mothers, but a few of them became domestics in Yankee households. Virtually all of these pioneers were

"two-boat" Irish—immigrants who came west after several years in the East or Canada.

In 1852 three brothers, Thomas, Walter, and Dennis Doheny, founded Minnesota's first Irish farming settlement at Jessenland. Tom apparently traveled the fifty miles up the Minnesota River alone from St. Paul that spring on the steamboat *Black Oak* and staked several claims at what became known as Doheny's Landing. He managed to clear enough land with hand tools to plant some potatoes, but after losing these to an early frost, he returned to St. Paul for the winter. The next year all three brothers were living on their claims in this lush green valley. By 1854 they had been joined by two hundred settlers, most of them Irish Catholics.

Bishop Joseph Cretin is credited with naming Jessenland for the biblical land of Gessen on a visit to the area in 1856. (According to Genesis, the patriarch Jacob led his descendants into Egypt when famine struck their homeland. Joseph, Jacob's son, was influential in the new realm and give his father that section of the country known as Gessen, the best land in all of Egypt.) This Irish settlement spread over much of Jessenland, Faxon, Washington Lake, and Green Isle townships. At its peak about 1900 it numbered some two thousand people.

The village of Green Isle was platted in 1881, and the present St. Brendan's Church was built the following year. This is the only church dedicated to the Irish saint in Minnesota. St. Brendan was abbot at the monastery at Clonfert, County Galway, in the fifth century, and supposedly discovered America with a group of Irish monks long before Columbus. The architect and contractor for St. Brendan's was John Lillis who had recently completed St. Michael's Catholic Church in Stillwater.

Built at a cost of twenty-five thousand dollars, St. Brendan's graceful spire rises 160 feet into the clouds. The main Gothic-style altar was made by a German Lutheran farmer, John Albers. Those people who contributed at least one hundred dollars to the building fund had their names inscribed on a scroll and placed inside an iron box in the cornerstone. One woman also remembered that parishioner Thomas McMahon, whose name was not included, dropped his picture into the box when the pastor, Father Timothy Ryan, wasn't looking.

Most of the Irish farming families have since moved from the Jessenland area where they have been replaced by Germans. As a rule, the Irish in America have become an urban rather than a rural people. Given the chance for an education, Irish young people flocked to the cities. The Germans, traditionally good farmers, tend to remain on the land. This is not to say that the Irish never prospered as farmers, however. Take the Currans, for example.

Tiny Green Isle made the front pages of Twin Cities newspapers in 1946 when Dan Curran was found dead of a presumed heart attack in the woods on his farm. Dan and his brothers, Tim and John, both of whom had died during the preceding year, had been farmers all their lives, but by living frugally the three had amassed a fortune. If this didn't in itself warrant so much attention, the fact that they hoarded a good deal of it at home did. As soon as Dan's body was discovered, guards were posted at the house, and a search for the money was conducted following the funeral. Almost twenty thousand dollars in gold coins (taken out of circulation during the Depression), along with another thousand dollars in silver, all of it buried in cans, was dug up in the cellar. One hundred sixteen thousand dollars in bonds and currency was found hidden under floor boards and throughout the house; one hundred sixty-five dollars in change was swept up in a closet. In all, counting money the Currans had in banks, the estate totaled a half million dollars.

 Jessenland's first Irish settlers are buried in this
hillside cemetery that dates to at least 1856,
behind the Church of St. Thomas. The breathtaking
view from this vantage point takes in the site of
Doheny's Landing on the Minnesota River.

There were also early Irish farming settlements in Dakota, Carver, and Le Sueur counties. Farther south, in the Mississippi Valley, others were located near Brownsville and Caledonia in Houston County, Chatfield in Fillmore County, and Rochester in Olmsted County. In Rice County, well ahead of Archbishop Ireland's later efforts, General James Shields organized the state's first Irish colony at Shieldsville in 1855.

Nationally known as a soldier and statesman, James Shields was born in County Tyrone, Ireland, in 1806, and came to this country at the age of sixteen. By the early 1830s he was practicing law in Illinois where he was also elected to the state legislature and later to the post of state auditor. During this time he became involved in a celebrated "affair of honor" with Abraham Lincoln. As a proud young Democrat, Shields was held up to ridicule in a series of letters in the *Springfield Journal* signed "Aunt Becca." When he demanded to know who had written them, the editor revealed that it was Lincoln's fiancee, Mary Todd. Characteristically, Lincoln assumed responsibility for the letters and Shields challenged him to a duel. The two met across the river in Missouri (because dueling was illegal in Illinois) ready to do combat with broadswords, but their seconds were able to halt any bloodletting. Lincoln instead apologized and the episode was ended.

Incredibly enough, in one lifetime General Shields managed to get himself elected to the United States Senate from three states, Illinois, Minnesota, and Missouri. He also distinguished himself in combat in three wars, the Seminole War in Florida, the Mexican-American War, and the Civil War. In the Mexican-American War, though wounded at Cerro Gordo and Chapultepec, Shields both times led his troops to victory. His command was the first to enter the City of Mexico and plant the stars and stripes in the halls of the Montezumas.

Following this conflict, and after being defeated for reelection to the senate from Illinois in 1855, General Shields came to Minnesota. He was one of the original proprietors of the townsite of Faribault. Ten miles northwest of Faribault, he laid out the townsite of Shieldsville for an Irish colony. Some of its first settlers were Irish immigrants who had served with him in Mexico. So many Irish farmers subsequently responded to his advertisements in eastern papers that most of Shieldsville's rich farmland was preempted by the next fall. Erin township filled and so did parts of Webster and Wheatland.

General Shields remained in Rice County about three years, but he soon became involved in other projects. (Certain colonists felt that he neglected their interests in favor of his investments in Faribault; there were also quarrels about an extra fee he charged on property deeds.) In 1857 he was elected to the United States Senate from Minnesota for a short term that ended in 1860, and after-

Temperance was a thing of the past for this group when this photograph was taken in John Ryan's Saloon in Green Isle about 1915. Ryan is the man behind the bar.

Green Isle was nearing the end of its heyday as a flourishing farming center when this photograph of the Mercantile Company and Post Office was taken in 1915. Thousands of Minnesotans claim family ties to early Green Isle residents.

wards he moved to California. During the Civil War, at Winchester, Shields was the only man to ever defeat Andrew Jackson in battle; his closing years were spent on a farm in Missouri where he lived until his death in 1879. There are statutes of General Shields in the Capitol in Washington, D.C., and in Minnesota's Capitol in St. Paul.

Shieldsville's Irish past is recalled in a charming local history, *Meet Shieldsville,* by Mary Hagerty which even includes its fairies and poockas. The first crop of boys in Shieldsville, she says, wore dresses and long curls until they were twelve years old. This was to fool the fairies. The fairies might steal male children, but they never bothered little girls. Sometimes, too, a healthy child was taken and a weakling left in its place. This was called a changeling.

A poocka is a spirit sent back from Purgatory because he or she has left some things undone on this earth. "Did you ever see a horse, or a dog, or a chicken that reminded you of someone you used to know? Well, ten to one, that's a poocka," explains Hagerty. They are obliged to hang around until prayers enough have been said to redeem their souls. But not all poockas are the real McCoy.

The story persists that there were once three nice old ladies, very pious, who lived together in Shieldsville and kept a lighted candle and a vase of flowers in front of a picture of their dead mother. A young neighbor named Eddie got the idea that this woman would make a fine poocka. He came often to visit the old ladies and talk about poockas and even brought them wood and flowers. Meanwhile, he noticed that their mother wore a frilled cap that looked like his mother's nightcap and had a scarf around her neck.

One night when the ladies were seated in front of the fireplace, they were startled by a rap at the window. Looking up, they caught just a glimpse of a white cap and shawl that reminded them of their mother. The apparition repeated itself every three days after that, and once it dashed through the house and blew out the candle. Still, the daughters never mentioned these happenings to the neighbors. They wanted it clearly understood that their mother was a saint in heaven.

His confidence soaring, Eddie asked the three if he could take a look at their chimney. He wouldn't want them to have a fire in the night, he said. They agreed, and Eddie completed his inspection, but he also left the ladder in place. That night a little white poocka was seen and heard on the roof beside the chimney playing "The Last Rose of Summer" on a mouth organ.

Imagine his surprise when he heard his father and mother and another man at the foot of the ladder, discussing what effect a shotgun would have on a poocka! Eddie made a hasty retreat down a drain pipe on the other side of the roof and hurried home. Later, when his mother asked him how he tore his new nightie, his only explanation was that "things like that just happen."

But nary a poocka has since appeared in Shieldsville.

This was Green Isle's first girls' basketball team, organized in 1910. Top row: Abby Clancy, Ella Murphy. Second row: Genevieve Nevin, Professor E. F. Joncas, Grace O'Meara. Third row: Elizabeth Murphy, Jenny McMahon, Margaret Kiernan, Ella Kiernan.

These sturdy gentlemen worked for the Garrick
& Murphy Ditching Company in Green Isle in
the early years of this century.

A procession of the Blessed Sacrament at St. Malachy's Church, built in 1878 in Clontarf, one of Bishop Ireland's colonies in Swift County.

BISHOP IRELAND'S COLONIES

By far the most important Irish colonization plan in Minnesota was carried out by Bishop John Ireland. Historian James Shannon termed it "the largest and most successful Catholic colonization program ever undertaken in the United States." Between 1876 and 1881, the prelate established ten rural villages and farming communities (De Graff, Clontarf, Graceville, Minneota, Ghent, Currie, Avoca, Iona, Fulda, and Adrian) in five western Minnesota counties (Swift, Big Stone, Lyon, Murray, Nobles) that are still flourishing Catholic centers.

Initially, Bishop Ireland hoped to better the lot of Irish immigrants living in eastern industrial slums by helping them to obtain their own farms. He was also eager to promote Catholic settlement in Minnesota. At the same time, both Minnesota and the newly-organized railroads that crossed the state were equally anxious to people the western prairies. Since it was altogether possible for good citizens to be practicing Catholics and likewise patronize the railroads, what was good for one was good for all in this case. The result was that church, state, and commerce frequently worked

hand in hand toward the rapid population of Minnesota.

In January, 1876, less than a month after he had been consecrated to the bishopric, John Ireland announced the establishment of the Catholic Colonization Bureau in St. Paul. This agency actively solicited Catholic immigrants for Minnesota from eastern states and from Europe. The bishop also said that he had signed a contract with the St. Paul and Pacific Railroad that named him its exclusive agent for all railroad lands in Swift County, about seventy-five thousand acres. (State and federal land grants allotted railroads alternate sections of land up to five miles deep on either side of their tracks.) His immediate plans were to bring two thousand immigrant families to Minnesota. This was the first of eleven similar contracts Ireland negotiated with five different Minnesota railroads during the next five years.

Bishop Ireland's lieutenant in the colonizing effort and the man he relied on to see it carried through was his close friend, Dillon O'Brien. Officially, O'Brien was executive secretary of the Catholic Colonization Bureau. Twenty years the bishop's senior, he was well-educated (at the Jesuit College of Clongowes in Ireland), a gifted writer, and a fluent public speaker. Above all, like John Ireland, O'Brien was a humanitarian.

Dillon O'Brien belonged to the minority of Irish Catholics born to prosperous circumstances in Ireland, but he had been ruined just the same. When the famines occurred, O'Brien and his wife, the former Elizabeth Kelly, and their four children were living at Fairfield, the family estate in County Galway. With tenant farmers no longer able to pay their rents, the O'Briens in turn could not satisfy their creditors, and the mortgage on Fairfield was foreclosed.

With little to call their own, the family emigrated to America, to Orchard Lake, Michigan, where Dillon had a distant relative. Taking whatever work he could find, O'Brien hired out as a laborer on the docks at nearby Detroit, and was sometimes able to supplement his income by lecturing. In 1857 he gladly accepted an appointment as teacher at the Indian school at La Pointe on Madeline Island, Wisconsin, where Bishop Frederic Baraga was operating a mission.

In the isolation of this outpost, once his classwork was completed, O'Brien began work on his first novel, *The Dalys of Dalystown*. The hero is an impoverished scion of an old family who comes to America and recoups his fortunes sufficiently to return to Ireland and regain his estate. This was a personal dream of O'Brien's, but one he never realized. *The Dalys of Dalystown* was published in St. Paul in 1866, and O'Brien followed it with three more novels, *Frank Blake* (1876), *Dead Broke* (1873), and *Widow Melville's Boarding House* (1881). In 1870 he opened a bookstore specializing in Catholic and Irish literature at 67 Seventh Street in St. Paul.

The O'Briens left Madeline Island in the early 1860s, but one son, John, who became a leading St. Paul lawyer, returned and built the first summer home on the island in 1895. Other family members followed his lead and a string of small frame cottages on the waterfront just east of the village dock became known locally as O'Briens' Row. For the past several years, Dillon's great-great-granddaughter, Jean Teisberg, has been curator at the historical museum on Madeline Island.

Born in Roscommon, Ireland, in 1818, Dillon O'Brien committed his life to seeing the Irish prosper in America. Archbishop Ireland called him "the true Christian philanthropist."

In 1865 Dillon brought his family (which now included six children, a seventh was born in Minnesota) to St. Paul where he became editor of the *Northwestern Chronicle,* the weekly diocesan newspaper. As such he was easily the most influential Catholic layman in the state. Using the paper as his forum, he frequently promoted the two causes closest to his heart: temperance and Irish settlement in Minnesota. In many quarters Irish immigration to the West was being seen as at least a partial solution to the insidious evil of insobriety which plagued too many urban Irish. "Give me temperance and a healthy immigration to land as levers," O'Brien promised, "and I will raise my people to the highest standards of citizenship."

O'Brien's arrival in St. Paul coincided with John Ireland's return from the Civil War. From their first meeting until O'Brien's death at the archbishop's residence twenty years later, their close friendship worked to the profound benefit of their fellow Irish. Both shared the same ideals and labored unstintingly to attain their common goals. Besides being a teetotaler (he had taken the pledge from Father Theobald Mathew while still in Ireland), O'Brien found the idea of Irish colonization so personally appealing that he moved his family to eighty acres of cheap, fertile railroad land he purchased near Litchfield in Meeker County in 1869.

Years later when the O'Briens moved back to St. Paul, the family's oldest daughter, Susan, married to Benjamin Cayou, an ex-soldier and a farmer, remained on the farm. At one time Dillon and his sons (three of whom became lawyers, one of them the mayor of St. Paul) owned three houses in a row on Lincoln Avenue in St. Paul. Dillon's descendants in the city and immediate area alone presently number in the many hundreds.

Bishop Ireland's railroad lands in Swift County (which included four townships, each six miles square) were quickly taken up by Catholic settlers beginning in 1876. Three years after its opening the colony embraced some two hundred thousand acres and the townsites of De Graff (named for a pioneer Minnesota railroad contractor) and Clontarf (after the Irish townsland near Dublin). A third colony was started in 1878 at Adrian in Nobles County, and was followed the same year in Murray County by Avoca. As it developed, Avoca divided into the settlements of Iona, Fulda, and Currie. Graceville (named for Bishop Grace), whose colonists bought land in Big Stone and Traverse counties, was established in 1878; and the final colonies, Minneota and Ghent in Lyon County in 1879 and 1881.

Dr. M. J. Egan, an avid hunter, pictured with his three children, Fabian, Dorothy, and Ian, in 1911, was Graceville's veterinarian.

Much to John Ireland's credit, since not all railroad land was equally fertile, either he or his agent, Major Ben Thompson, personally inspected every parcel of land before recommending it to prospective buyers. Once assured of the worth of a tract, Ireland had Dillon O'Brien write a brochure describing its location, type of soil, anticipated yield per acre, and the average rainfall typical of the area. The first of these pamphlets (*An Invitation to the Land: Reasons and Figures*) appeared in 1877 and was addressed to the victims of the recent general labor strike in the East.

"Those who own land own the country," O'Brien wrote. Surely life on the open "prairie with herds and granary and free homesteads" was preferable to living in "dark, unhealthy tenement rooms, doing the slavish work of the docks and streets, with no hope of advancement." He also pointed out that while Catholics living in the East had been slow to move West for fear they would be bereft of clergy, Bishop Ireland was providing priests for his colonies. Settlers could reap the benefits of the land and still maintain their close ties with the church.

Certainly this was no pie-in-the-sky offering. O'Brien's final section, "A Chapter for All to Read," tells of the hardships to be expected, the toil, primitive facilities, and limited social life on the prairie. But the opportunity was there, he declared, for a man to realize a comfortable return on his labor in a few years while enjoying the independence of being his own man. Minnesota winters were not all as bad as they were usually made out to be either, said O'Brien. His exact words (now venerated as cliche) were: "It's a dry cold, and really quite bracing." He urged his readers to think of winter in Minnesota as a time for "warm robes, a light cutter, a fast horse, and tinkling sleigh-bells." During the winter of 1878, O'Brien and a German-speaking priest also toured eastern cities where they spoke enthusiastically of the colonies to Catholic audiences in English and German respectively.

Bishop Ireland was seeking only those men who had been farmers or who were willing to take up farm life, O'Brien stressed. Another important qualification, and one that eliminated many of the very people the bishop hoped to help, was that each settler bring at least four hundred dollars to see him through the first year. This would cover the cost of materials for a small house (with two doors and two windows), food, fuel, oxen, a cow, and tools, but not the price of the land which could usually be mortgaged for a ten-year period. While O'Brien was deluged with letters from the truly poor who wanted to come to the colonies, there simply were no funds to assist most of them. The modest budget of the Catholic Colonization Bureau (which was financed largely through land sale commissions from the railroads) was barely sufficient to cover office expenses, salaries, and printing costs.

Vincent O'Brien was the son of St. Paul attorney John O'Brien, and a grandson of Dillon O'Brien. The John O'Briens lived at One Crocus Hill (where young Vincent once tried to keep goats and chickens in the attic). Vincent later married Dr. Arthur Gillette's only daughter, Margaret, and built the home at 90 Crocus Place that is still occupied by family members.

Most of those who came to Bishop Ireland's colonies were Irish, but French, German, Belgian, and English immigrants also answered his invitation. All of them, though, were Catholic. The settlements were religious centers where the local priest was both the temporal and spiritual leader. Besides erecting a church, he saw that a frame house was built and five acres of land broken for each incoming family. He was an expert on the best type of seed for the area and when to plant it, and could explain the intricacies of tax and real estate laws as well.

When grasshoppers swooped down on De Graff for a second time in 1877, one Father McDermot was the first to attempt to eradicate them. Traveling to Willmar, the nearest division point on the St. Paul and Pacific, he arranged for the purchase of newly-patented "hopperdozers" from St. Paul. These large steel scooplike contraptions were filled with tar to trap the insects, then pulled along the fields behind two horses.

In several of the colonies, the St. Paul and Pacific constructed large emigrant houses to shelter arriving families. At Avoca, the parent colony of the Catholic settlement in Nobles and Murray counties, Bishop Ireland built Colony House for the same purpose. Once homes were put up for the settlers, these temporary structures were moved farther west or converted to other uses. For his part, the bishop was not interested in getting into the hotel business and made every effort to attract small businessmen to the colonies. An article in the *Northwestern Chronicle* in 1877 mentions the need for a lawyer, a machinery dealer, and a hotel keeper in De Graff. A little later, the paper advised that "De Graff needs a general store."

Like western railroad towns in general, the Irish colonies were efficiently platted but austere. This plainness was in sharp contrast to the grand and beautiful house of worship Bishop Ireland built in each community, often on the shore of a lake. He also encouraged residents to spend time and money fixing up their homes and lawns. (Newcomers who had lived in stone cottages in Ireland were sometimes slow to grasp the economic and psychological value of a fresh coat of paint, he noticed.)

One disappointment to John Ireland was that he was never able to bring any significant number of destitute Irish to Minnesota. Nor was there any great influx of Irish laborers from the East; many of these no doubt also lacked the necessary capital. Mostly, the colonies filled with farm families from the Midwest to New England. As it turned out, settlers who were able and willing to pay their own way, rather than relying on assistance from the bishop or other sources, were generally more successful as colonists.

The parish of St. Patrick in Edina dates to 1857 when a log church was built in the Irish community known as the Cahill Settlement. The frame church, pictured, was built in 1888; the present church opened in 1961.

Bishop Grace constructed this imposing episcopal residence for St. Paul clergy in 1860. It adjoined the city's new and third Cathedral, built on the corner of Sixth and Wabasha streets in 1858. The house was considered palatial in its day but lacked even ordinary bathroom facilities until 1896; coal or wood stoves sufficed for heat until a steam heating plant was installed in 1910.

THE CONNEMARA AND SWEETMAN COLONIES

In 1880 twenty-four indigent Connemara families from County Galway that Bishop Ireland settled near Graceville in Big Stone County proved complete failures on the land. These people were victims of the famine that followed a poor harvest in Ireland in 1879. Concerning their plight in their homeland, one parish priest had written: "This locality is not fit for human habitation. Not more than a third of the present population can live in any sort of comfort on the land." If some of these people could be relocated, the others might better survive.

Though he had serious doubts that these peasants who had been fishermen and garden farmers could make a go of large-scale farming, John Ireland agreed to bring fifty such families to Minnesota. Some of the expense was borne by private donations solicited through the *Northwestern Chronicle.* Each family received a 160-acre farm (at a cost of four dollars an acre financed by the railroad) with a small frame house and furnishings, clothing, farming implements, seed, and credit at Graceville for a year's supply of food.

From the onset it was an ill-fated proposition. Dillon O'Brien went to Boston to meet the emigrant ship, and at first sight of this destitute band (which numbered more than three hundred persons), found his worst fears confirmed. His son, Thomas O'Brien, wrote later that the "kindly but visionary" priest who had selected these people in Ireland had chosen "from the most congested districts not the competent, but the incompetent; not the industrious but the shiftless; a group composed of mendicants who knew nothing of farming, and were entirely unfitted to cope with life upon the American prairie."

Once they arrived in St. Paul, Bishop Ireland found employment for forty-five young men and thirty-five young women, the latter probably as domestics, that they might help support their families. When the rest of the settlers reached Graceville, he asked the families already established there to take the immigrants into their homes until the new houses were ready. This was where the trouble started. The earlier Graceville residents found the newcomers dirty, uncouth, and offensive. One woman even refused to allow such people in her house. Still, the Connemaras were in their homes soon enough and their future looked promising. Wheat was selling in these years for a dollar a bushel and the rich, black farmland around Graceville yielded as much as twenty bushels an acre.

The first summer passed uneventfully; many of the Connemara men worked as day laborers on neighboring farms or laying track for the western extension of the St. Cloud and Lake Traverse Railroad which was advancing towards Graceville from Morris. But the storm was gathering. In September, when Bishop Ireland visited Graceville, he failed to find any sign of want among the Connemaras, but the tone of their conversation disturbed him. Some clearly preferred laboring jobs (which would never provide enough income to pay for their farms) to working the land. They were also dissatisfied with their wages which ranged from a dollar and a half to two dollars a day. The upshot was that the bishop instituted a public works program in Graceville financed by the diocese. All comers were paid a dollar a day, but any man who didn't sign up or make himself useful on the colony farms would find his credit for provisions cut off in Graceville.

It was apparent that the Connemaras were content to let the bishop support them if need be. He had brought them here, after all. Some had sold the seed given them by the colonization bureau and others had just not planted it. Still others had sold their farming tools. When winter came, it was unusually early and severe and the Connemaras were unprepared for it. While they had been told to sod the exterior foundations of their houses to protect against the cold, many of them had not done this. Before long, when the group was reported to be in dire straits, Bishop Ireland issued an appeal for funds for their relief in St. Paul. During the worst of the winter he was able to send them six hundred dollars a month. Dillon O'Brien went to the colony to distribute the money, but later disclosed something of the real situation:

"Last winter when the snow was too deep for horses and sleighs, the other farmers in the colony bought flour...and drew it by hand on sleds over the snow to their homes. The Connemara men would not take the flour away, although to them it was a free gift. Some of the farmers, when a sum was offered them to carry the flour to the homes of the Connemara men, said they were willing enough to make a dollar, but that they would not turn their hands to benefit such a lazy people."

Archbishop John Ireland purchased this house at 977 Portland Avenue for his archiepiscopal residence in 1892. Shortly before he died in 1918, the archbishop moved to the Amherst Wilder mansion at 266 Summit Avenue, directly across from the new Cathedral. Sisters of St. Joseph who taught at the old St. Luke's grade school (now part of the William Mitchell College of Law) afterwards used the Portland Avenue house as a convent.

The sorriest part of it was that the Morris newspaper listened to complaints from the Connemaras and printed reports of their neglect at the hands of Bishop Ireland and Dillon O'Brien. These charges were repeated in the *St. Paul Pioneer Press* amid growing sympathy for the unfortunate colonists. When a subsequent investigation in Graceville showed that some of these people had hidden food and clothing to make their suffering appear greater, the truth won out. The *Pioneer Press* carried an explanation of the fiasco which cleared Bishop Ireland and the colonization bureau of any responsibility for the hardships which the Connemaras had brought on themselves. Before the year was out, Bishop Ireland arranged transportation for the group to St. Paul where he found jobs for some of them with the railroads, Most of them settled in St. Mary's parish on the flats along Phalen Creek under Dayton's Bluff which became known as the "Connemara Patch."

Thomas O'Brien believed that the stress and utter frustration of dealing with the Connemaras may well have shortened his father's life. Dillon O'Brien died suddenly on a Sunday morning in February, 1882, at the old gray stone episcopal residence on Sixth Street where he had stopped on his way to Mass at the Cathedral to see John Ireland. The bishop was likewise heartsick at the failure of the Connemara colony. His secretary, Monsignor Humphrey Moynihan, wrote that "the disastrous record of the Connemaras caused untold pain and humiliation to the best benefactor Catholic colonists had in America.... Indeed, Archbishop Ireland confided to Mr. William O'Neill, one of the most prominent members of the Graceville community, that the incident was the greatest grief of his life."

A second Irishman who sought to establish a colony for impoverished Irish families in western Minnesota was John Sweetman. A wealthy landowner in County Meath, and the scion of a family who had been brewers in Dublin for several generations, Sweetman was troubled by the suffering he saw among his countrymen from famine in these years. The first thing he did was to start a series of drainage projects on his property to provide employment. Men walked seven and eight miles, he found, to work for him, and he could not hire all who came. When he traveled to Minnesota in 1880 to meet with Bishop Ireland, it was because he wanted to bring several dozen Irish families to America.

With Dillon O'Brien as his guide, Sweetman toured the Irish colonies and examined the cropland in each place The area he decided on was around Currie, north of Avoca, where he arranged for the future purchase of ten thousand acres of railroad land, Back in Ireland, he interested a group of well-to-do Catholics in organizing a stock company that would supply the venture capital. This was the Irish-American Colonization Company with headquarters in Dublin. Sweetman invested twenty thousand pounds sterling in the enterprise (which was capitalized at one hundred fifty thousand pounds sterling) and acted as its managing director without pay. The prospectus he prepared explained that the company would purchase land in suitable localities and place settlers on it, providing them with what they required for a fair start. A mortgage would be held on the land, implements, stock, and farm effects until the settler repaid the debt with fair interest in installments. With any luck, stockholders could expect a return on their investment.

The first group of nearly two hundred colonists, most of them penniless, arrived in Currie in May, 1881. The company had advanced their passage money and agreed to sell each family eighty acres of farmland (at an average price of six dollars an acre) with no payment expected until after the second year's harvest. Small frame houses were built for the families and they were supplied with oxen, farm equipment, seed, and food. If more could be done for them, Sweetman didn't know what it was. His mistake instead had been in being too generous. Of the forty-one families who came to Currie from Ireland in 1881, only twenty-five were left two years later.

A year's experience taught him, said Sweetman, "that people would profess to be anxious to settle on farms for the sake of obtaining a passage to that paradise of an Irish labourer's imagination—the United States. But having arrived there, they would not remain on their farms, but would go to the cities for the sake of escaping the debt incurred for their passage." Single men who brought their sisters to keep house for them made the most unreliable settlers of all. Unused to this kind of drudgery, the sisters soon went to the cities where domestic positions paid wages, and their bachelor brothers abandoned the farms. This first year cost John Sweetman heavily. To prevent the same thing from happening to others who had invested in his company, he bought up ninety percent of the firm's stock.

The next year when Sweetman brought a second group of families to this country, it was with the stipulation that they paid their own passage. Many of these left the colony just the same. The first years on a prairie farm were backbreaking ones; unless a man had a personal investment to protect, said Sweetman, he found it hard to resist the temptation to leave with the proceeds of his first harvest (which had cost him nothing). These new farmers were also of the opinion that since the company had done so much for them, they must be doing a great deal of good for it. This they naturally resented. According to Sweetman, their discontent stemmed from too much "spoon-feeding." He likened them to "spoilt children."

Beginning in 1883 Sweetman had no choice but to insist that prospective colonists pay ten percent down on their farms with the balance due in nine years. This was the year that Currie's fortunes began to turn around. Sweetman pointed out that during the first winter settlers had used the best cord wood for fuel because they could get it on credit. Later, when it came to paying cash for it, they cut and burned hay in their stoves instead. Sweetman himself remained in Murray County until 1892. Eventually he recouped much of his initial loss by selling colony lands to German and French Catholics who came from Illinois.

In 1908 Archbishop Ireland wrote to Sweetman in County Meath, Ireland: "I have visited Murray County and went through it from one end to another in an automobile. What a change from the days of oxen and slow horses! I was particularly delighted with Currie. A magnificent school-house has been built near the Church and the attendance of pupils is quite large. I met many of the old colonists—especially Mr. Mooney. All without exception are delighted that they remained in Murray County. All are prosperous and revere your name and memory."

John Sweetman concluded that "as a scheme for helping Irish immigrants to settle on land in America, my work was a failure, but as establishing a Catholic Colony on the prairies, it seems to have been a success."

The John Murphy & Company elevator was
built in Kilkenny, Minnesota, about 1900. It
burned in 1923 and was rebuilt, but was closed
down and dismantled a few years later. Kilkenny is
the only town of that name in the United States. One
of its first settlers, Dennis Doyle, a schoolmaster
from County Kilkenny, Ireland (where he taught
young John Ireland), named it for his homeland.

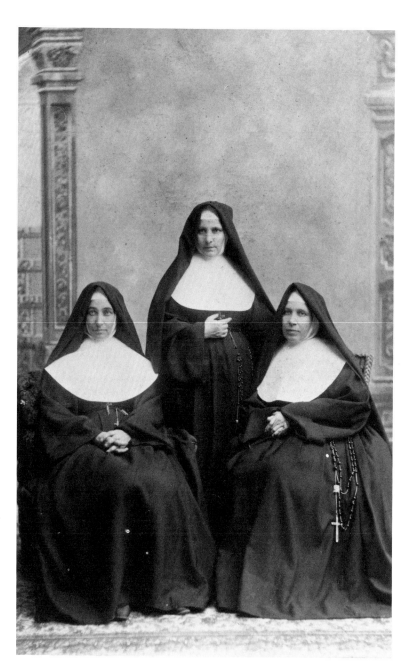

A family of nuns: Sister St. John (Eliza Ireland), Mother Celestine (Ellen Howard), and Mother Seraphine (Ellen Ireland), about 1885. Sister St. John entered the convent ten years after her older sister, Mother Seraphine, and was superior at Holy Angels Academy in Minneapolis for many years. She died in her forties of tuberculosis at St. Joseph's Academy in 1897. Her funeral Mass was said in the school's chapel by her brother, the archbishop.

THE ARCHBISHOP'S SISTER

Ellen Ireland was the archbishop's younger sister, and more than that, his female counterpart. At sixteen, while John was in France studying for the priesthood, she took the habit of the Sisters of St. Joseph of Carondelet and the name Sister Seraphine. There was never much doubt that she was cut from the cloth of leadership. For a period of thirty-nine years beginning in 1882, she served as Mother Superior of the sisters' St. Paul Province (Minnesota, North Dakota, and South Dakota). During her tenure the order opened forty-eight new houses including more than thirty schools and five hospitals. Ultimately she accomplished her dream of founding a college for women.

Her story is set against the backdrop of St. Joseph's Academy in St. Paul, Minnesota's first girls' school (1851) and the state's first high school (1853). In the fall of 1852, the year they arrived in St. Paul with their families, ten-year-old Ellen and her cousin of the same age, Ellen Howard, were enrolled at the school. One of their classmates was Mary Mehegan who married James J. Hill. (Long afterward the Hills' daughter, Clara Hill Lindley, recalled: "In later life my mother and Mother Seraphine would reminisce over their schooldays and would laugh over a dramatic performance, the trial scene from the 'Merchant of Venice.' The costumes were the best white muslins with a black velvet bodice, with Van Dyck points to distinguish the male characters.")

Both Ellens were in the school's first graduating class in 1858, and both immediately made plans to join the Sisters of St. Joseph. Years earlier when Bishop Cretin had come daily to the Ireland home to bring communion to eight-year-old Richard Ireland who was dying of typhoid fever, he had told the girls: "You *must* be sisters. The Lord has need of you." On December 8, the Feast of the Immaculate Conception, they were formally accepted into the order as novices. Seventeen-year-old Sister Seraphine was teaching at St. Joseph's Academy before the year ended; within three years she was the directress. After that, except for temporary assignments to other convents, the school was her lifelong home.

At one point, in 1872, Sister Seraphine was sent to Hastings to open St. Teresa's Convent where she taught and served as mother superior. Ignatius Donnelly, who lived in nearby Nininger, sent his daughters to the school, and the sisters were always welcome at his home. On one such occasion that Mother Seraphine was fond of remembering, she said that a box of books arrived for Donnelly from his sister in Philadelphia, Eleanor C. Donnelly, then widely known as a Catholic poet. Donnelly excused himself to open it and returned presently with a volume for her which he had hurriedly inscribed, "To Mother Seraphim from Brother Cherubim." She had laughed, she said, and told him, "There are a few things you will have to do before you can be called Brother Cherubim."

Following the Hastings assignment, from 1877 to 1882, Mother Seraphine was superior at the Catholic orphanage for girls in St. Paul's Lowertown. A contemporary sister wrote: "She was greatly beloved by both the Sisters and the orphans. No work was too hard or too menial for her to do. Being of a strong and robust constitution she usually bore the heaviest part of the burden and was first in laundry, kitchen, and at the scrubbing. She slept in the dormitory with the Sisters and led the common life in all things."

In 1882 when she was first elected superior of the St. Paul Province, she was forty years old, with twenty-four years of experience as a sister of St. Joseph to draw upon. Until now, despite having few resources other than their own dedication, the sisters in this province had fared amazingly well. They had increased in number from four pioneer sisters in 1851 to more than 160 strong some three decades later. By this date they had established eight houses or institutions: St. Joseph's Academy, St. Joseph's Hospital, and the girls' orphanage in St. Paul; St. Anthony Convent, Holy Angels Academy, and the boys' orphanage in Minneapolis; St. Teresa's Convent in Hastings; and St. Joseph's Convent in Stillwater. But now the province was embarking on a period of unparalleled growth under Mother Seraphine.

Her first project was St. Agatha's Conservatory which opened in 1884 in a rented house on Tenth Street behind St. Joseph's Hospital in St. Paul. Two years later it moved to the Judge Palmer mansion, which the sisters purchased for fifty thousand dollars, on Cedar and Exchange Streets opposite the old State Capitol. At its inception, Mother Seraphine named her cousin, Sister Celestine (Ellen Howard), by then an able administrator in her own right, mother superior in charge of St. Agatha's. She remained in that position until her death in 1915; during her thirty years there she also coordinated the parochial school system.

This is St. Mary's Academy in Graceville about 1892. The teacher is Sister Inez. St. Mary's was a two-room school; the younger children were taught downstairs, while a second teacher held classes for the older pupils upstairs.

St. Agatha's was intended as a home for the sisters who taught in the parochial schools and it eventually housed more than ninety of them (some of whom walked considerable distances to their classes whatever the weather). Beyond that, it became nationally recognized as a music conservatory and was unique among the sisters' institutions. The income derived from art and music classes and other enterprises conducted there became a much-needed source of support for the always hard-pressed community.

Dating to their earliest years in France, the Sisters of St. Joseph have a long-standing reputation as students and teachers of art and music. An appreciation of the fine arts has been part of their cultural heritage. One of the first expenditures in any new convent was usually for a piano; revenue from lessons helped sustain the houses. At St. Agatha's the success of the art and music programs exceeded even Mother Celestine's high expectations. According to a full-page advertisement in a musicians' directory of the Twin Cities for 1912-1913, St. Agatha's offered classes in piano, organ, violin, zither, theory, history of music, harmony, mandolin, guitar, banjo, counterpoint, voice culture, elocution, languages, painting, china decorating, and drawing.

Several of the sisters at St. Agatha's became expert at copying classical paintings, working at first from masterpieces in Twin Cities collections, then in Chicago and Montreal museums. In 1908 Mother Seraphine allowed three of these artists, Sisters Marie Teresa, Anysia, and Sophia, to go to Europe for two years where they studied and worked in galleries in Italy, France, and Germany. They returned home with copies of Renaissance paintings by such masters as Andrea del Sarto, Correggio, Murillo, and da Vinci. One of the most prized pieces was a copy of Raphael's ''Madonna of the Chair,'' copied at the Pitti Gallery in Florence and placed in a replica of the original frame. Some of these remarkable paintings were sold to the sisters' patrons, but many others were kept for their convents. Until the school closed in 1971, an outstanding collection hung in the classrooms, halls, parlors, and chapel at St. Joseph's Academy.

Irish politician Ignatius Donnelly, relaxing on the porch of his home in Nininger with his children and grandchildren in this 1890s photograph, was the best-known Minnesotan of his time. A superb and energetic orator, he stumped the state time and again, championing agrarian causes. Putting issues above party politics, he was in turn a Democrat, Republican, Greenbacker, Granger, Farmers' Alliance supporter, Populist, and Fusionist.

St. Agatha's Conservatory was housed in the former Judge Palmer residence on the corner of Cedar and Exchange streets in downtown St. Paul until 1910, when the sisters built a new seven-story brick building on the site. The school closed in 1962; the brick building is now known as Central Manor and operates as a home for disabled adults.

Certainly the money never came easily at St. Agatha's. The sisters were constantly at work teaching classes, painting and selling pictures—miniatures, still lifes, particularly floral arrangements, and religious subjects—or hand painting and firing their popular chinaware. Many a sister walked home from teaching school only to go to work in an art room making carefully hand-painted cards or exquisite imitation roses. In 1904 when the sisters were selling calendars door to door, one tired nun returning to St. Agatha's after selling her quota was sent out again because she had done so well.

Nor was much of the money ever spent on the sisters. They truly lived in poverty, and often in need, while what they earned went to carry on the expanding work of the province. After St. Agatha's, during the next thirty years Mother Seraphine opened a network of parochial schools at the rate of one a year, many of them in the western Minnesota communities colonized by Bishop Ireland. The state was being rapidly populated by wave after wave of Catholic immigrants, and Mother Seraphine intended to bring education and at least some measure of refinement to their prairie settlements where both were in short supply. The sisters also staffed five new hospitals, three of them in North Dakota— St. John's in Fargo, St. Michael's in Grand Forks, and Trinity in Jamestown—along with St. Mary's in Minneapolis and St. John's in Winona.

In 1903 the cornerstone was laid for Derham Hall, the first building on the campus of the College of St. Catherine. Mother Seraphine had first made plans for a Catholic college for women in St. Paul in the 1880s, but these were scrapped during the national financial panic in 1893. In 1900 Archbishop Ireland published a special edition of *The Church and Modern Society,* a collection of his sermons and addresses, and assigned the proceeds to the sisters' college fund. The nuns peddled the books door to door and town to town, and eventually raised sixty thousand dollars. Hugh Derham, the well-to-do Rosemount farmer for whom Derham Hall is named, gave the sisters an additional twenty-five thousand dollars on the archbishop's advice.

Even more than money, the convents needed sisters, and Mother Seraphine had a definite talent for recruiting young women. For one thing, she had a magnetic personality that drew people to her; for another, she was persistent. From the parishes where they taught, her sisters regularly brought girls to meet her. Once she decided her visitors had a vocation, they usually ended up joining the convent, whether they originally had any intention of doing so or not.

Many of the nuns also came from Canada and Ireland. Mother Seraphine's sister, Julia (the only one of the six Ireland children to marry), was the wife of a teacher, Charles McCarthy, who had moved to St. Paul from the Canadian Maritime Province of Prince Edward Island. Late in the 1890s, when he learned that Mother Seraphine was looking for young women to train as teachers, he told her she could find them in plenty on the island. Mother Seraphine is said to have lost little time in putting on her shawl. She obtained a letter of introduction from her brother, the archbishop, asked her cousin, Mother Celestine, to accompany her, and headed for Prince Edward Island. There the pair went from parish to parish, telling of the great need for teaching sisters and inviting girls to join the order.

Over a period of several years beginning in 1899, some eighty-five young women from Prince Edward Island entered the order. One of the earliest Canadian sisters remembered dressing as a postulant in a black dress and wearing a veil for the train trip to St. Paul. As she recalled, Indians and members of religious orders rode free on the Canadian trains. Additional prospective nuns from Canada and Ireland were brought to St. Paul by priests, and sometimes a sister could obtain permission to go home for a visit if she promised to return with a niece or a cousin. While there had been 162 sisters in her province when Mother Seraphine became superior, she saw that number increase to 913 nearly a half century later in 1930.

Customarily Mother Seraphine called on all of her convents once a year. Sometimes she arrived by train, other times by a horse-drawn buggy. Her visits were always eagerly anticipated social events, announced in the newspapers. There was usually a purpose for her trips, but one sister wrote that while "her word was law, the charm of her personality generally left her subjects liking the law." She had a fine sense of humor and might delight her audience, including the parish priest who had stopped by, with amusing anecdotes such as her account of the Lutheran deaconess who asked her how she kept her sisters in at night.

This was hardly the extent of her travels, however. It is sometimes jokingly said (at least in Catholic circles), "Join the convent and see the world," and Mother Seraphine did just that. Besides business trips to New York, Boston, Philadelphia, and Chicago, she attended biennial conferences at the St. Louis mother house, and traveled to Montreal and Quebec City on religious pilgrimages. The trip that gave her the most pleasure was a voyage to Europe late in 1908 in a party of six that included Archbishop Ireland. On December 8, the fiftieth anniversary of her own reception into the order, she and the others made a pilgrimage to the mother house in Lyons, France, which had sent the first Sisters of St. Joseph to the United States (in 1836). In Rome they were received in a private audience by Pope Pius X who blessed the hundreds of rosaries Mother Seraphine presented—one for each of the sisters in her province.

St. Joseph's Academy, founded in 1851, has been at its present site at 355 Marshall Avenue since 1863. After 120 years (during which time it also served as a novitiate, the sisters' provincial house, and a retirement home for older nuns) the academy closed in 1971. It has been designated a National Historic Site; the buildings are currently used by the Christ Household of Faith, a religious group that practices a communal life style.

Mother Seraphine was known as the archbishop's sister, but it seems apparent that even at the pinnacle of John Ireland's career, he was still Ellen Ireland's brother. Several sisters later recalled interactions that they had observed: "When the archbishop came to visit us at St. Agatha's or...[St. Joseph's] Academy, she always came too. She saw to it that she was there. ...And she'd sit beside him and prompt him if he...forgot something, and he'd do the same to her if she forgot." Mother Seraphine's concern for the diocese's priests was another link with her brother. "A real friend and confidante to priests," she served them as "kind of a go-between" with the archbishop. If the priests could not get the archbishop to go along with their plans, or if they had a misunderstanding with him, "they'd bump themselves right over to [St. Joseph's] Academy, where she was...and she would say, 'You go home and I'll take care of my brother.' " The two Irelands also shared a family resemblance. As one nun put it, Mother Seraphine was of average height, heavy set, with "a jaw like the archbishop's."

In 1921, when she was seventy-nine, Mother Seraphine retired from active leadership. (She had been reelected to a three-year term a dozen times, but changes in church law made in 1918 allowed superiors to finish their current terms, but thereafter limited the tenure of religious offices to six years.) After that, although the provincial headquarters were moved to the campus of the College of St. Catherine, Mother Seraphine remained at St. Joseph's Academy. She died there at the age of eighty-eight in 1930, seventy-two years from the time she had entered the Sisters of St. Joseph. Her entire family had preceded her to Calvary Cemetery. She was the last of the Ireland generation that had led Catholic affairs in Minnesota for more than half a century.

After Ignatius Donnelly's death (on January 1, 1901, the first day of the twentieth century), his home in Nininger, built in the 1850s, stood empty for many years and fell into disrepair. Attempts by early preservationists to save it proved futile; it was razed in 1949.

Scott Fitzgerald as a child with his father, Edward Fitzgerald. Edward was descended from several prominent Maryland families; his great-great-grandfather was a brother of Francis Scott Key, for whom young Scott was named.

A PRODIGAL SON

After Scott Fitzgerald died in 1940, Princeton University refused to buy his papers for $3,750. The school felt no responsibility to subsidize the down-and-out widow of this hack writer from the Midwest—even if he was an alumnus, commented its librarian. A grand total of seventy-two copies of *all* his books sold that year, and Fitzgerald seemed slated for oblivion.

Quite the opposite happened, of course. Fitzgerald's star began soaring the very next year when Scribner's published his unfinished novel, *The Last Tycoon.* It didn't sell paticularly well (thirty-five hundred copies), but the critics loved it. Calling it Fitzgerald's "Unfinished Symphony," reviewer Stephen Vincent Benet was right on the mark when he wrote: "You can take off your hats now, gentlemen, and I think perhaps you had better. This is not a legend, this is a reputation—and, seen in perspective, it may well be one of the most secure reputations of our time."

Arthur Mizener of Northfield, Minnesota, wrote the first Fitzgerald biography, *The Far Side of Paradise,* in 1951. Since then more than forty books and hundreds of articles have been published about the colorful St. Paul writer. His books are not only once again best-sellers (one edition of *The Great Gatsby* sold well over three million copies), they are classroom staples. His popularity is also worldwide. While *Gatsby* alone appeared in foreign language editions (French, German, and Swedish) in his lifetime, since 1950, Fitzgerald's books have been translated into thirty-five languages.

Born in St. Paul on September 24, 1896 (in the San Mateo Flats at 481 Laurel Avenue), F. Scott Fitzgerald was no less than the first major American novelist of Irish descent. His maternal grandfather was a prosperous St. Paul wholesale grocer, Philip McQuillan, born in County Fermanagh, Ireland. When he died at the age of forty-three in 1877 from Bright's Disease complicated by tuberculosis, McQuillan's fortune exceeded a quarter-million dollars. His oldest daughter, Mollie, married to Edward Fitzgerald, was

Scott's mother. It was her inheritance, when Edward failed as a businessman, that kept the Fitzgeralds on the fringes of St. Paul's fashionable Summit Avenue neighborhood. The Fitzgeralds lived at a half dozen different addresses in the area, but the official F. Scott Fitzgerald residence is a rowhouse his parents rented at 599 Summit Avenue. His first novel, *This Side of Paradise,* was written in one of its third-floor rooms in 1919.

"In regard to the man himself," his friend Edmund Wilson wrote about Fitzgerald for the *Bookman* in 1922, "there are perhaps two things worth knowing, for the influence they have had on his work. In the first place, he comes from the Middle West.... The second thing... is that Fitzgerald is partly Irish and that he brings both to life and to fiction certain qualities that are not Anglo-Saxon. For, like the Irish, Fitzgerald is romantic, but also cynical about romance; he is bitter as well as ecstatic; astringent as well as lyrical.... He is vain, a little malicious, of quick intelligence and wit, and has an Irish gift for turning language into something iridescent and surprising."

Fitzgerald's hometown turns up frequently in his fiction. Several of the Basil Duke Lee stories (in which the hero is a thinly-disguised version of the author), for instance, recall his adolescent years in St. Paul. Published in the late 1920s, these include "The Scandal Detectives," "A Night at the Fair," "The Captured Shadow," and "Forging Ahead."

Two earlier stories set in St. Paul, "Winter Dreams" and "The Ice Palace," concern eager young men (again like Fitzgerald) whose love lives suffer in the city. In "Winter Dreams," Dexter Green first glimpses Judy Jones and the life led by the rich while he caddies at Black Bear Lake (an obvious play on White Bear Lake where wealthy St. Paulites built their summer homes). Green makes his fortune with a string of laundries in St. Paul and joins the University Club, but when Judy jilts him, he abandons the city and goes East.

"The Ice Palace," much in the same vein, is about Harry who invites his Georgia fiancee, Sally Carrol, to visit him in St. Paul during Winter Carnival week. It'll be like fairy-land to you," he promises her. Once in Minnesota, though, despite the festivities, Sally is miserable. Unaccustomed to snow and cold, and at one point terrified when she finds herself alone in the ice palace with no lights, she forsakes Harry and returns to Georgia. (In this last piece Scott was anticipating Zelda's reaction in similar circumstances. Her first and only winter in Minnesota was spent in St. Paul following the birth of the couple's daughter, Scottie, in 1921, and she hated it.)

🍀 The golden boy of the jazz age he created, St. Paul's F. Scott Fitzgerald was the first Irish Catholic to become a major novelist in this country.

The best-known (and most sentimental) of Fitzgerald's descriptions of St. Paul appears in *The Great Gatsby*. One of his cherished memories, Nick says, is of "coming back West" from college on the train at Christmastime: "That's my Middle West—not the wheat or the prairies or the lost Swede towns, but the thrilling returning trains of my youth, and the street lamps and sleigh bells in the frosty dark and the shadow of holly wreaths thrown by lighted windows on the snow. I am part of that, a little solemn with the feel of those long winters, a little complacent from growing up in the Carraway house in a city where dwellings are still called through decades by a family's name."

The fact of Fitzgerald's Irishness, on the other hand, is perhaps less noticeable in his work. Reaching as he was for the golden ring, it is possible that he soft-pedaled his ancestry to avoid being stereotyped. It is true, too, that he was not particularly proud of being Irish. For all the McQuillan fortune, Mollie was still a dowdy woman and Scott was sometimes ashamed of her in his youth. (For a time about the age of nine he nursed the fantasy that he was a foundling of royal blood who had been dropped on the Fitzgerald doorstep.) Nevertheless, Fitzgerald's prose is intimately bound up on several levels with his Irish upbringing.

There is first of all his tendency to flavor his work with a pinch of Irish seasoning here and there. When Dick Diver in *Tender Is The Night* tries to conceal his embarrassment for Rosemary Hoyt, his face moves "first in an Irish way." In describing Charles Wales in "Babylon Revisited," Fitzgerald mentions "the Irish mobility of his face. . . ." The cast in *This Side of Paradise* includes Beatrice O'Hara, the hero's mother who is an extravagant Irishwoman. One critic even argues that all of his main characters, no matter their outsides, are really the Irish author himself.

More than that, Fitzgerald's Irish background is basic to understanding his view of life as an artist. Malcolm Cowley explained that "like [Finley Peter] Dunne, he had been accepted into the ruling Protestant group, and unlike Dunne he wrote about that group, so that his Irishness was a little disguised, but it remained an undertone in all his stories, it gave him a sense of standing apart that sharpened his observation of social differences." Coming as he did from a "lace-curtain" Irish Catholic home, and moving into the inner circle of the Protestant establishment, Fitzgerald wrote with a keen sense of double vision. As both outsider and insider he used his enormous talent to mock the American Dream. No other American writer has better depicted his chosen subject. It seems only fair to suggest that his Irish soul indeed made a difference.

F. Scott Fitzgerald became one of the greatest writers of all time. Somewhere along the way he also turned his back on St. Paul. In 1934, after he and Zelda had spent several years in Europe and were living in the East, he wrote to Marie Hersey Hamm (a former childhood sweetheart) in St. Paul: "I no longer regard St. Paul as my home any more than the eastern seaboard or the Riviera. This is said with no disloyalty but simply because after all my father was an easterner and I went East to college and I never did quite adjust myself to those damn cold Minnesota winters. I was always freezing my cheeks, being a rotten skater, etc.—though many events there will always fill me with a tremendous nostalgia."

St. Paul fighter Tommy Gibbons (on the left),
a one-time heavyweight title contender, spars
in a local gym with his brother, Mike Gibbons, who
fought as a middleweight and a welterweight,
about 1915.

THE FIGHTING IRISH

"There is no branch of athletics," declared poet John Boyle O'Reilly in 1888, "in which Irishmen, or the sons of Irishmen, do not hold first place in all the world." This boast was very close to the truth; nineteenth-century Irish athletes excelled in baseball, track and field, and wrestling. Their unquestioned specialty was prizefighting.

In Minnesota, Irishmen dominated the fighting scene well into the twentieth century, though formal bouts were infrequent in the state's early years. Rivermen, railroaders, and other laborers were continually brawling in the streets anyway. One of the first fights on record took place in present-day West St. Paul in 1869 when "Chicago Red" Mulowney battered a fighter named Johnson for a purse of one hundred dollars. Mulowney was all of fourteen years old at the time. That same year, two Irishmen named Johnny Hannon and Mike McDonald were arrested before a scheduled bout could take place.

Another fighter of the bareknuckle era, "Red Handed Mike" O'Connor, claimed the middleweight championship of the region around 1870 and evidently managed to stay out of jail. Staying out of jail was not always easy. Prizefighting was illegal in Minnesota until the time of World War I. Promoters had a couple of options: they could avoid the law by keeping the fight's site a secret until the last minute, or they could persuade authorities that the event was merely an "exhibition." The time-honored traditions of bribery undoubtedly also helped many a fight to come off.

The roll of prominent Minnesota boxers of the last century reads like an Irish genealogy: Dickie Moore, Tommy Hogan, Pat Killen (who allegedly once bit off an opponent's ear), Charley Gleason, Danny Needham (who lost a seventy-six-round bout in Minneapolis to Chicago's Tommy Ryan), the brothers Joe and Danny Sheehy. For all the punishment they gave and received, their names are forgotten to history. One area heavyweight, however, Patsy Cardiff of Minneapolis, earned a lasting place in the record books when he became one of only three men to gain a draw against the legendary John L. Sullivan. The fight took place on January 18, 1887, at the Washington Rink in Minneapolis.

The last bareknuckle champion and the first champion of the modern era, Sullivan was ideally suited to the task of confirming the public's worst fears of the Irish. "They may boast of their vaunted John L. Sullivans," said an anti-immigrant pamphlet of time, "but one clear-eyed Yankee boy with a Winchester repeater could take care of a dozen such." Sullivan was a walking affront to Victorian morality. He abandoned his wife to live openly with a chorus girl. He drank "Black Velvet," a mixture of champagne and whiskey, by the bucket, and was often so drunk in the ring that his trainers had to guide him through the ropes. By 1887, his dissipations made him seem ripe for defeat and Minnesota's Cardiff appeared a likely man to take the title.

Some ten thousand people—the largest crowd ever assembled under one roof in Minneapolis to that time—cheered wildly when Cardiff entered the arena to take on the champ. He may have needed their enthusiasm; the *Minneapolis Tribune* reported that "panic stood in Patsy's eyes and walked abroad on his pale cheeks." But it was Cardiff who "drew first blood" (an important gambling point). When he forced Sullivan to the ropes in the second and sixth rounds, the crowd sensed an upset in the making.

Instead, referee Pat Sullivan (no relation) called the fight a draw at the end of six rounds. Neither Cardiff nor the crowd knew until he made his announcement that Sullivan had fought at least half the fight with a broken arm. (One Sullivan admirer said it happened in the first round when John L. landed a blow "to the point of Patsy's chin.") Cardiff's backers claimed they had been robbed. But Sullivan was unimpressed. "He ain't no gentleman," pronounced the champion. Under today's rules, the title would have gone to the Minnesotan.

Boxing's popularity flagged locally for a time after this, though a title match between middleweight champion "Ruby Robert" Fitzsimmons and Australia's Jim Hall was scheduled for St. Paul on July 22, 1892. At the last minute, authorities bowed to pressure from Archbishop Ireland and other civic leaders and banned the fight. That autumn the legislature tightened the rules against boxing, and the public taste for action sports turned to wrestling matches.

Born in 1887, Mike Gibbons began his notable ring career at the age of twenty, several years before boxing was legalized in Minnesota. Gaining local fame during these "undercover" bouts, he afterwards became one of the cleverest boxers in prizefighting history.

This was Green Isle's first basketball team in 1910, organized by Father James Doyle, pastor at St. Brendan's, and Professor E. F. Joncas who taught at the local school. Father Doyle had been the basketball coach at the College of St. Thomas before coming to Green Isle. Standing: Bravy Meyers, Professor Joncas, Joe Corcoran. Seated: Joe Martin, Harry Davitt, Raymond Davitt, James Kiernan. Eddie Dwyer is holding the ball.

Around 1910, however, promoters began to take advantage of the legality of boxing in nearby Wisconsin by organizing train and auto excursions to cards in Hudson. About the same time, two superb fighters emerged in St. Paul: Mike Gibbons and Mike O'Dowd, the sons of immigrants from Counties Mayo and Galway respectively. Their successes and those of their fighting brothers helped turn St. Paul into one of the fighting capitals of the country.

Mike ''The Harp'' O'Dowd (one of several boxing brothers) became Minnesota's only world champion in 1917 when he defeated Al McCoy for the middleweight title. Even so, Mike Gibbons is generally conceded to have been the best fighter in the state's history. Though he never had a title bout, during his career Gibbons faced no fewer than seven champions. Tommy Gibbons, Mike's younger brother, gained international fame on July 4, 1923, when he fought fifteen rounds with heavyweight champion Jack Dempsey in a winner-take-all bout in Shelby, Montana. The fight is considered one of the great bouts of the century, but Gibbons unfortunately came home with nothing.

The sophistication and scientific approach of the Gibbons brothers did much to elevate boxing to a new level of respectability in this area. This was a new age of the sport, immeasurably distant from the violence of the previous century, and the end of the Irish hegemony. Tommy Gibbons went on to serve as sheriff of Ramsey County for twenty-four years—a position which, only a few decades before, would have required him to jail his prize-fighting colleagues.

Ignatius Aloysius O'Shaughnessy achieved spectacular success as an independent oil promoter. His flair for philanthropy ensured his lasting reputation.

KING OF THE WILDCATS

Minnesota's oil-rich Ignatius Aloysius O'Shaughnessy didn't believe in success stories. "When I read about the poor boy who shoveled snow to make his first dollar and slept in a coal bin to go to school, it gives me a pain," he told a reporter in 1945. "Young men succeed because they are in the right place at the right time, if they have character," he held. "Character is everything. There's no road to success through the front door of a bar or poolroom."

The youngest of thirteen children of Irish immigrant parents, O'Shaughnessy parlayed a talent for sniffing out oil into one of this state's largest fortunes. In 1973 *Corporate Report* magazine estimated his net worth at one hundred ten million dollars. The Minnesota philanthropist was also a leading benefactor of the Catholic Church in this country and abroad. Chief among the recipients of his largess were his alma mater, the College of St. Thomas in St. Paul, and the University of Notre Dame in South Bend, Indiana. There was no question that he enjoyed playing Santa Claus.

On one occasion, O'Shaughnessy contributed four million dollars for the construction of the Ecumenical Institute for Advanced Theological Study, midway between Jerusalem and Bethlehem. Intended for both Christian and non-Christian scholars, the center commemorates Pope Paul VI's historic meeting with Greek Orthodox Ecumenical Patriarch Athenagoras in the Holy Land in 1964. Recalling a meeting he had with Pope Paul and Father Theodore Hesburgh, the president of Notre Dame, O'Shaughnessy said: "I told Hesburgh [who was translating] to tell His Holiness to get off his pants and get at it right away because people forget soon. Hesburgh had a rough time trying to say that in Italian, and in a different way, to the Pope. But the deal was made." Pope Paul afterwards conferred the title of Papal Count on the St. Paulite.

Ignatius Aloysius O'Shaughnessy was born to John and Mary Milan O'Shaughnessy in Stillwater, Minnesota, on July 31, the feast of St. Ignatius Loyola, in 1885. "By the time I arrived," he explained, "mother had run fresh out of all the regular names like John, James, and Joseph, and being a good Catholic, she went to the Calendar of Saints. So I became Ignatius." He chose his second name himself when he was confirmed as was customary at the time. St. Aloysius is the patron saint of boys, but the nun who taught him at St. Michael's grade school in Stillwater also had that name. He told her he picked it "because [Aloysius] was the boys' saint and because I liked her too." His nickname was Nashe.

His father, John O'Shaughnessy, from County Galway, had learned the shoe-making trade in Milford, Massachusetts, before coming to the booming lumbering town of Stillwater in 1857. He brought ten or twelve shoemakers with him and these men mainly made boots for lumberjacks. The O'Shaughnessy boot and shoe store was located at 210 Chestnut Street until John's death in 1910. Nearby, John built a large white frame residence for his sizable family at 703 South Third Street. (This house is still standing but has been made smaller.)

Young Nashe attended local Stillwater schools and played baseball and football on the side. One summer he worked as a laborer in one of the sawmills that lined the riverbank. This was to toughen himself up for football, he remembered. It was hard work, twelve hours a day, six days a week. The pay was $1.40 a day. In September, 1901, following in the footsteps of four of his brothers, he boarded a train for Collegeville and St. John's University. It was a beautiful place, three miles out in the country from the station, but too far from home for him. The next spring he switched to St. Thomas in St. Paul where he became captain of the football team and star halfback.

After graduation, Nashe worked briefly in his brother John's insurance firm in Houston, but the job lacked appeal for him. He stayed only long enough to get a grubstake so that he could prospect for oil in Oklahoma. Owing something to Irish luck, no doubt, he struck oil with his first well near Blackwell in 1910. This was only the beginning. Well after well produced for him, and according to the legend that grew up around him, none of O'Shaughnessy's wells ever ran dry. In the oil fields, he was "king of the wildcats."

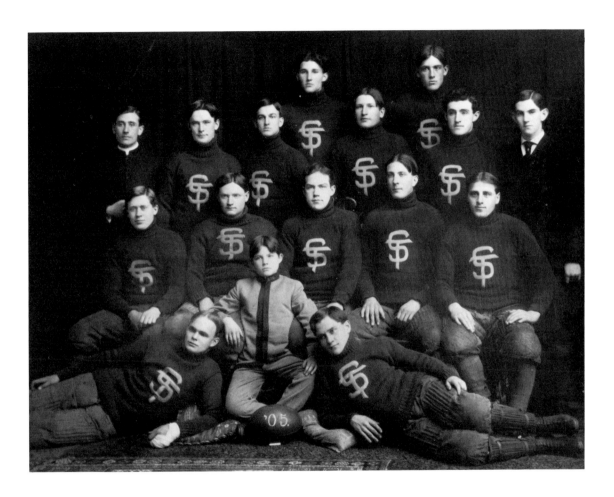

Nashe O'Shaughnessy, second row center, captained the St. Thomas football team in 1905 during his senior year.

O'Shaughnessy founded the Globe Oil and Refining Company in 1917, and later, the Globe Pipeline Company, and Lario Oil and Gas Company. His first refinery was a small one at Blackwell, but this was soon followed by larger installations at that site and two others. When he began construction of a million-dollar refinery at McPherson, Kansas, in 1932, he was reportedly the largest individual refiner in the United States. (The press also credited him with "blazing the trail out of the depression" that year.) O'Shaughnessy cited "the rapidly increasing demand for high octane, anti-knock gasoline" as the reason for the McPherson plant. He also promised that "no expense will be spared in our efforts to continue production of the finest gasolines and oils for the modern motorist."

O'Shaughnessy's wife for fifty years and the mother of his five children was the former Lillian Smith of St. Paul. The couple met aboard the riverboat *Capitol* on a Mississippi cruise sponsored by St. Mark's parish while Nashe was still in college. Father William Hart married them in that church in 1908. The O'Shaughnessys lived at 705 Summit Avenue in St. Paul, but wintered in Florida where private tutors were engaged for their children. Lillian once protested that people ought to have only enough money to pay their expenses, but Nashe only laughed: "What shall I do? Turn off the faucet?"

What O'Shaughnessy could do and did do was to give away large portions of his fortune. Beginning in 1939 his gifts to St. Thomas helped finance a library, an athletics building, a football stadium, and an education center, all of which bear his name. At the College of St. Catherine in St. Paul, he built the O'Shaughnessy Auditorium (where he and Lillian attended performances of the St. Paul Opera Company and the Minnesota Symphony Orchestra). During the early 1950s, when he was president of the board of trustees at Notre Dame, he contributed more than two million dollars for a liberal arts college at the Indiana school. This also earned him Notre Dame's annual Laetare Medal. In announcing the selection, Father Hesburgh remarked that "[O'Shaughnessy's] benefactions appear to be the largest made by any single person in the history of Catholic education in the United States."

In addition, there were substantial gifts to non-Catholic institutions including Carleton College in Northfield, Macalester College in St. Paul, Shattuck School in Faribault, and the University of Minnesota. Local hospitals counted on O'Shaughnessy's generosity and he funded medical research. He also helped countless friends and relatives meet their expenses. It would be impossible, a member of his staff said, to total what he gave away because the gifts were so numerous. In 1957 Lillian O'Shaughnessy built the housekeeping home for girls at the Home of the Good Shepherd in St. Paul that is named for her.

Another side of Nashe O'Shaughnessy never gave up his love of sports. In 1955 when he became an owner of the Cleveland Indians, he called it a boyhood dream come true. "I think it is the youthful ambition of everyone interested in athletics to someday own a major league baseball team," he said. "I know it was mine." He was disappointed, he told the press, that Minneapolis and St. Paul had not been able to resolve their differences concerning a new stadium site, but he hoped to see major league ball in the Twin Cities in the near future.

In 1958 the O'Shaughnessys celebrated their fiftieth wedding anniversary with a trip to Ireland. Together with several other Irish Americans, O'Shaughnessy had recently purchased an eight-thousand-acre estate, Lakes of Killarney, in County Kerry. Asked by a newsman what he intended to do with the place, he said that he "could not possibly improve on it"—that it was perfectly beautiful as it stood. There was no truth to the rumor, he insisted, that there was oil on the property.

The O'Shaughnessys spent five weeks in the manor house, Rosse Castle, and afterwards traveled to County Galway where they located O'Shaughnessy Castle and met residents who remembered the family. Topping off their trip, they made a pilgrimage to Rome where both were decorated for their generous works by Pope Pius XII. It was the trip of a lifetime, but the year did not end happily for the pair. Shortly after their return to St. Paul, a special anniversary Mass, set to be celebrated at St. Mark's by Archbishop William Brady, was cancelled when Lillian was hospitalized. She had suffered from heart disease for several years and died a few months later at Golden Beach, Florida.

In 1966 at the age of eight-one, O'Shaughnessy wed a second time. His bride was Blanche Finn, a widow and a long-time friend, who lived in Cocoanut Grove, Florida. She had no children and had always been a housewife, she said in an interview. Bishop James Shannon officiated at the private ceremony which took place in the chapel of the Chancery at 266 Summit Avenue. One of O'Shaughnessy's sons and his wife stood up for the couple.

Up until the time of his death (in a Miami hospital) on November 21, 1973, O'Shaughnessy maintained a top-floor office in the First National Bank Building in St. Paul. His business interests were scattered throughout the United States, but his roots were in Minnesota. He was also a man of deep family convictions. "Money or fame doesn't count," he reiterated time and again. "Family is all we have. Food, shelter, and clothing can be bought with money, but the important things cannot." Monsignor Terrence Murphy, president at St. Thomas said of him: "While some people are great because of the money they make, with Mr. O'Shaughnessy it was the other way around. He made money because his ability and character made him a great man."

Archbishop John Ireland's funeral procession on October 2, 1918, was the largest ever seen in St. Paul. Eight archbishops, thirty bishops, twelve monsignors, seven hundred priests, and two hundred seminarians took part in the ceremonies. Bishop Thomas O'Gorman celebrated the Pontifical Mass of Requiem; John Ireland was buried in Calvary Cemetery beside his predecessors, Bishops Cretin and Grace.

GRAND FINALE

In a superb recent essay, "Message of the Irish Character," Minnesota poet Eugene McCarthy described the five great loves of the Irish people.

The first of these is their great love of country, he says, "for the soil of Ireland, for its towns and its people." Like St. Columcille whose greatest punishment was that he could never again set foot on Irish soil, McCarthy suggests that we, too, all feel the pang of exile when away from the homeland.

Secondly, the Irish have a great love for religion—"for the things of the spirit, for the faith." Witness the comparative ease with which St. Patrick converted Ireland. That he was able to do so without spilling so much as a drop of martyr's blood can only mean that he found the Irish spirit ready and willing to accept Christianity.

The third great love of the Irish is their love of learning. It was the Irish who kept alive "the flame of knowledge and the pursuit of truth" during the Dark Ages, "when in all parts of the world, learning was despised and trod upon." Irish monks fostered art and literature in isolated monasteries; Irishmen were among the finest teachers at the court of Charlemagne (about 800 A.D.).

The Irish also have a deep-rooted love of political freedom. Ancient Gaelic law forbid the seizure in a man's home of his books, his sword, or his harp. Books symbolized his intellectual and spiritual freedom, while the sword bespoke his political freedom. The harp stood for all things to which the human heart aspires.

The fifth great love of the Irish is their love of poetry and song. As late as the fifteenth and sixteenth centuries, English rulers singled out "bards, minstrels, rhymers, and genealogists" for special penalties; poets were blamed for inciting the Irish lords and gentlemen to rebellion and other crimes. Cromwell's soldiers at the time of the invasion smashed the harps they found on the walls of Irish cottages.

McCarthy was right as far as he went. These five loves indeed mark the Irish heart. But the Irish are large-hearted and have a less serious side to their nature as well. Given the goings-on in St. Paul come St. Patrick's Day, it seems fair to conclude that the Irish, at least on this side of the ocean, also love a parade.

Some people think that the reason St. Paulites let out all the stops on St. Patrick's Day has to do with the fact that they have had their fill of a long winter. Possibly so. Marching (and a pint of green beer) will do wonders to warm up the blood. But when these same people contend that St. Patrick's Day is little more than a convenient excuse for celebrating the arrival of spring, they are kidding themselves. Spring rarely sallies forth in Minnesota in mid-March (no matter what the calendar says). The Irish, to boot, would likely muster the same kind of exuberance should St. Patrick's Day fall at any other time of the year.

According to an article in the *Pioneer,* the first St. Patrick's Day parade on record in St. Paul was held in 1851: "The Sons of the Emerald Isle, and our citizens generally, joined in an impromptu celebration of the anniversary of St. Patrick, on Monday last. The Stars and Stripes were elevated to the peak of the liberty pole in front of the Central House; but unfortunately, the wind being high, the tall mast was broken off, some twenty feet from the ground. The flag was then raised upon the stump and a salute fired. Speeches were then made." After supper, "a procession was formed, headed by a band of music & numbered some three hundred, which marched through the principal streets, visiting the residences of many of our citizens."

Two years later, on March 17, 1853, upwards of three hundred men wearing green scarves thrown over their shoulders and shamrocks in their hats assembled for a parade after Mass at the Cathedral on Sixth and Wabasha streets. This parade wound through the streets to the accompaniment of fife and drum, and included an impressive contingent from the Irish Catholic Temperance Society. Bishop Cretin found it a "strange thing!" that the Irish wanted "to celebrate pompously the day of St. Patrick," but he was glad all the same that "no one complains about the sermons in French and English." The Catholic population of St. Paul was still predominantly French as was the bishop.

🍀 The Kilkenny chapter of the Ancient Order of Hibernians posed for this St. Patrick's Day photograph about 1910. Front row: Michael Healey, George Keough, Peter E. Byrne, John McGeough, Father Carey, Father Reilly, J. B. Smith, Tom Trainor. Second row: J. F. McCarthy, James McCabe, Michael Doran, Andrew Balfe, Tom Lawler, Professor Maloney, Ed Cunningham, Frank (Cully) Crosby. Back row: James Greer, Phil Lawler, Myles Brennan, James Higgins, Richard Murphy, James Furlong, Martin Hagerty, Charles Cooney, William Sheridan, William Murray, Patrick Keough.

These early parades were orderly, if spirited, processions. While the St. Paul newspapers called attention to occasional disturbances caused by drunken Irishmen (the *Daily Minnesotian* in July, 1856, for example, told of the Irish tough named Dillon who, having had a "drop of the creature" cowed the entire St. Paul police force), much of the Catholic community was in favor of total abstinence. On St. Patrick's Day, 1856, the Benevolent Society of the Sons of Erin staged a lively parade and later a dinner where the toasts were drunk in cold water. John O'Gorman, Richard Ireland's friend and the father of the future Bishop Thomas O'Gorman, was president of the Society and presiding officer. Bishop Cretin and ex-Governor Ramsey were among the two hundred and fifty guests, both men and women.

During the Civil War era, St. Patrick's Day festivities became more extravagant. Following High Mass at the Cathedral, numerous Irish marching groups in green-trimmed garb fell in behind the Great Western Band for the annual parade. They might stop at the Sisters of St. Joseph's convent and orphanage (to the utter delight of the children) and call on the governor or mayor for speeches.

At least a half dozen times between 1862 and 1871, either at the bishop's house or the Opera House, Father John Ireland delivered stirring St. Patrick's Day addresses as well. Hailed by the local Irish as a rhapsodic talent, the young priest aroused his listeners to pride and anger as he recounted the glories and agonies of Irish history; Ireland was likened to Israel as a chosen nation. His purpose was to bolster Irish self-esteem, often at low ebb during the immigrant years, and to encourage his countrymen to pull themselves up by their bootstraps.

Separate parishes also scheduled St. Patrick's Day entertainments, usually musical programs or plays, in the evening. Dillon O'Brien penned a play about Robert Emmett for such an occasion and he and his sons performed in others. Sometimes all the parts were taken by men and boys because Father Augustin Ravoux, the vicar general of the diocese, was opposed to girls appearing on stage. Nor was Father Ravoux the only arbiter. Thomas O'Brien, Dillon's son, remembered others:

This picturesque group is the Green Isle "Harp Orchestra," which hired out for local parties and dances, about 1915.

"Once, after many rehearsals of a play in which I was supposed to be re-united with a long-lost daughter, Father Shanley, then pastor of the cathedral, told me there must be no kissing on the stage! I had enjoyed the rehearsals, as the young lady who took the part of the daughter was quite dear to me; but when the evening of St. Patrick's Day arrived and I was confronted by a group of austere clerics, my nerve gave out and I contented myself with shaking hands with the girl!"

St. Patrick's Day celebrations brought out the Irish in outlying communities as well. In 1867 seven hundred Irishmen attended a supper and song fest in Rochester. A few years later members of seven temperance societies from Goodhue and Wabasha counties met for the day in Lake City in 1875. In Green Isle, where St. Patrick's Day has always ranked after Easter and Christmas as the most important feast day of the year, St. Brendan's parishioners added a beauty contest to the agenda in 1882. Helen O'Brien was chosen the winner; her prize was a rocking chair. Later on, it was not uncommon for a hundred Green Isle townsmen to don the full regalia of the Ancient Order of Hibernians for their annual parade.

By the turn of the century, though, it seems that the parade in the capital city was beginning to get out of hand. In 1901 the Hibernians arranged special railroad rates to St. Paul for St. Patrick's Day with the result that four thousand men took part in the parade. By all accounts, it was a parade to end all parades. That it apparently did just that is somewhat ironic. There is no mention of a parade in St. Paul in 1902; the next year the Irish in the city reportedly celebrated St. Patrick's Day "very quietly and religiously." Archbishop Ireland had called a halt to what he saw as "midnight orgies."

More than a half century later, the St. Patrick's Day parade was revived in St. Paul by downtown businessmen in 1967. St. Patrick fills the role of pied piper for a day as the city is given over to merry-making. The bacchanal than ensues approximates the Mardi Gras with a coat of green gloss. While most of the marchers are family groups who carry name banners, thousands of noisy onlookers line the parade route. Many of the latter are likely to be inebriated and a good lot of them are not even Irish. Following the parade, local bars fill to the gills with mostly young people who prolong the revelry well into the evening. (Minneapolis, though it boasts a Scandinavian image the rest of the year, has also held its own St. Patrick's Day parades of late.)

This was John Ryan's Saloon in Green Isle shortly before prohibition caused its demise. Green Isle resident Dolly Brazil identified the men as James Welch, Pat Brazil, Dan Meyers (seated), a transient, Pete McDonald, _____Davitt, _____ Hannon (one arm), Tom Welch, John Ryan, Tom Ryan, Gilbert Corrigan, and Myles Slavin.

Not all of the Irish in St. Paul favor the parade. Some feel the impression it creates smacks too much of the stereotypical drunken, if fun-loving, Irishman. (Marchers, for their part, generally shrug off this objection; they enjoy identifying with their extended families.) As an alternative in some instances to this type of demonstration, increasing numbers of Minnesota's Irish are joining one or more of the state's many Irish political, social, and cultural organizations.

The Ancient Order of Hibernians, a mutual benefit society formed in Minnesota in 1879, is the oldest of these. The women's auxiliary dates to 1894. (The first new chapter of the Ancient Order of Hibernians in Minnesota in fifty years was organized in Jessenland in 1980.) Irish political groups active in Minnesota in recent years include Minnesota Irish Northern Aid, the Minnesota Irish National Caucus, the Liam Mellows Irish Republican Club (IRC), and the Irish Progressive Club. Socially-oriented organizations such as the Twin Cities Irish-American Club, the Minneapolis Irish Study Club, St. Paul's chapter of Comhaltas Ceoltoiri Eireann, and the Irish Music and Dance Association of Minnesota all promote Irish culture.

St. Paul can also claim the Irish American Cultural Institute, the largest organization of its kind in the world. Founded by Dr. Eoin McKiernan, a former professor of English at the College of St. Thomas, the Institute publishes *Éire-Ireland,* the senior Irish journal in the western world; sponsors lectures and performances by Irish writers, artists, and academics; and has produced more than fifty half-hour television programs on various aspects of Irish culture. It also makes annual awards to Irish artists and writers, and underwrites projects such as the "Irish Way" which enables high school students to travel and study in Ireland.

Princess Grace of Monaco was International Chairman of the Institute during her lifetime. In June, 1983, Dr. McKiernan became the first American awarded a life membership in the 252-year-old Royal Dublin Society in Ireland. This was in recognition of the significant role the Institute has played in furthering an appreciation of Irish culture in America. Irish Books and Media, the largest distributor of Irish books in this country, is also affiliated with the Institute.

Staff Major Emmett McCarthy leads the Old Guard of the Brian Boru Irish Pipe Band during the St. Patrick's Day parade in St. Paul in 1981. McCarthy was born in County Cork, Ireland, in 1922, learned music in the Irish army, and came to this country in 1958.

Since 1980 the Minnesota Irish Festival has also been an annual (and highly popular) event in St. Paul. It takes place in the fall at the Civic Center and features two days of nonstop entertainment by both Irish and Irish American groups. Pat Gallivan and his Gallivanters, well-known to patrons at Gallivan's in St. Paul in the 1970's, were on the 1983 program. So were the Mooncoin Ceili Dancers, a local troupe that has studied in Ireland. Complete with Irish films, Irish food, and Irish crafts and imports in the bargain, the festival is a well-balanced tribute to Irish ways.

The conclusion to be drawn is that Minnesota's Irish are taking a fresh look at themselves. A good part of this reawakening stems from the efforts of Eoin McKiernan and fellow Irishmen who are revitalizing the Irish image. The trick was in defrocking the familiar stage Irishman; if the Irish are taking their very Irishness more seriously, that is exactly what McKiernan has in mind. In Minnesota, Irish pride is especially well-placed. It comes as no surprise that the Irish contribution to this state has been substantial. Except for the Irish immigrant families and their descendants, Minnesota history would read very differently.

BIBLIOGRAPHY

Berger, John Gerald. *A History of St. Brendan's Parish, The Village of Green Isle and Minnesota's First Irish Settlement.* Privately published, 1966.

Bruccoli, Matthew J. *Some Sort of Epic Grandeur.* New York: Harcourt Brace Jovanovich, 1981.

Castle, Henry A. "General James Shields," in *Minnesota Historical Society Collections,* 15:711-730 (1915).

Graham, Sister Clara. *Works to the King: Reminiscences of Mother Seraphine Ireland.* St. Paul: North Central Publishing Co., 1950.

Hagerty, Mary L. *Meet Shieldsville: The Story of St. Patrick's Parish, Shieldsville, Minnesota.* Privately published [1940]. Reprinted, Lonsdale, Minnesota: Bendickson Printing, 1974.

Hurley, Sister Helen Angela. *On Good Ground, The Story of the Sisters of St. Joseph in St. Paul.* Minneapolis: University of Minnesota Press, 1951.

Johnston, Patricia Condon. "Reflected Glory: The Story of Ellen Ireland," in *Minnesota History,* 48:13-23 (Spring, 1982).

Kane, Patricia. "F. Scott Fitzgerald's St. Paul: A Writer's Use of Material," in *Minnesota History,* 45:141-148 (Winter, 1976).

McCarthy, Eugene J. *Complexities and Contraries: Essays of Mild Discontent.* New York: Harcourt Brace Jovanovich, 1982.

Martens, Sister Elizabeth Marie. *Academy for a Century, A History of St. Joseph's Academy Located in St. Paul, Minnesota.* St. Paul: North Central Publishing Co., 1951.

Moynihan, James H. *The Life of Archbishop John Ireland.* New York: Harper & Brothers, 1953.

O'Brien, Thomas D. *Dillon O'Brien: A Minnesota Pioneer.* Privately published, 1933.

O'Brien, Thomas D. *There Were Four of Us or, Was It Five.* Privately published, 1936.

O'Fahey, Charles Joseph. "John Ireland's Rhetorical Vision of the Irish in America." Master's thesis, University of Minnesota, 1973.

Reardon, James Michael. *The Catholic Church in the Diocese of St. Paul.* St. Paul: North Central Publishing Company, 1952.

Regan, Ann. "The Irish," in *They Chose Minnesota* (edited by June Drenning Holmquist), St. Paul: Minnesota Historical Society Press, 1981.

Shannon, James P. "Bishop Ireland's Connemara Experiment," in *Minnesota History,* 35:205-213 (March, 1957).

Shannon, James P. *Catholic Colonization on the Western Frontier.* New Haven: Yale University Press, 1957.

Shannon, William V. *The American Irish.* New York: MacMillan Publishing Co., Inc., revised edition, 1966.

Smith, Alice E. "The Sweetman Irish Colony," in *Minnesota History,* 9:331-346 (December, 1928).

Sweetman, John. *Recent Experiences in the Emigration of Irish Families.* Dublin: M. H. Gill and Son, 1883.

Sweetman, John. "The Sweetman Catholic Colony of Currie, Minnesota: A Memoir," in *Acta et Dicta,* 3:41-65 (July, 1911).

Besides these sources, I used two type-scripts by Sister Ann Thomasine Sampson: *The Ireland Connection* (1982) and *A Guide to CSJ Places of Historic Interest in Minnesota and North Dakota* (1983). Sister Ann Thomasine also helped me locate information pertinent to Mother Seraphine (Ellen Ireland) in the oral history interviews she has conducted for her community. All of this material is at St. Joseph's Provincial House, St. Paul.

The complete files of the *Northwestern Chronicle,* which provide a detailed account of Bishop Ireland's Catholic colonies in Minnesota, are preserved in the archives of the Catholic Historical Society, St. Paul. I also used the Irish American Colonization Company Papers and the O'Shaughnessy Papers at the Minnesota Historical Society Archives, St. Paul.

This book was designed by Dale K. Johnston.
The production consultant was Rohland W. Wiltfang.
The typestyle used throughout the book is Optima.
The paper is Northwest Mountie Matte.
This book was printed and bound by
Colwell/North Central Inc. in Saint Paul, Minnesota.